Animals of the Old Testament

Written by
Janet K. Warren

Illustrated by
Rebecca Prato

'Who teaches us more than the beasts of the earth, And makes us wiser than the birds of heaven?' Job 35:11

AuthorHouse™ LLC
1663 Liberty Drive
Bloomington, IN 47403
www.authorhouse.com
Phone: 1-800-839-8640

© 2013 Janet K. Warren. All rights reserved.

No part of this book may be reproduced, stored in a retrieval system,
or transmitted by any means without the written permission of the author.

Published by AuthorHouse 12/18/2013

ISBN: 978-1-4918-4017-7 (sc)
978-1-4918-4018-4 (e)

Library of Congress Control Number: 2013922929

Any people depicted in stock imagery provided by Thinkstock are models,
and such images are being used for illustrative purposes only.
Certain stock imagery © Thinkstock.

This book is printed on acid-free paper.

Because of the dynamic nature of the Internet, any web addresses or links contained in this book may have changed since publication and may no longer be valid. The views expressed in this work are solely those of the author and do not necessarily reflect the views of the publisher, and the publisher hereby disclaims any responsibility for them.

Dedicated to my mother Doreen, who I still miss every day, my father George, who I'm so glad we get to spend more time together with, when he isn't globetrotting, my two wonderful daughters Alysse and Kaitlyn who I couldn't be prouder of and of course Cavan, my life partner and best friend who, God love him, puts up with me.

'But now ask the beasts and they will teach you; And the birds of the air, and they will tell you." Job 12:7

Miriam the Dove and Noah

"And of every living thing of all flesh, you shall bring two of every sort into the ark, to keep them alive with you; they shall be male and female"   GENISIS 6:19

A very long time ago, in fact it was well over 2000 years ago; there lived a lovely little white dove named Miriam.

Miriam lived in the beautiful olive tree behind the home of Noah and his wife Emzara. Every day Noah or Emzara would set out seeds to feed Miriam and often, they would chat with Miriam. They spoke of how disappointed they were with everyone they met. Everyone was so very wicked and did not pray to God every day, like they did.

Both Noah and Emzara were very kind people and would even pray in their garden when the weather was good. Miriam liked to hear their prayers and knew how kind and wonderful God was.

One day, Noah told Miriam of a flood that God was sending and that he had been asked by God to build a huge ship called an ark. God had told Noah that the ark must be big enough for all of his family and two of every kind of animal in the world. Noah asked if Miriam would help him to gather the animals when it was time to load the ark.

Miriam knew that this was a very important job and now, Miriam had Ezra, who was a mate for her. Ezra was also very kind and gentle and Noah told Miriam how happy he was to have Ezra helping Miriam to gather the animals, when the ark was ready.

Miriam had also met the three strong sons of Noah and Emzara. Ham, Shem and Japheth were going to help with the building of the huge ark. Miriam knew how very happy God would be to have all of them building the ark. Ham, Shem and Japheth and their wives would also be on the ark with Noah and Emzara as well as Miriam and Ezra.

It was a lot of work to build something so big, but all of them worked very hard every day except Sunday, while Miriam and Ezra flew overhead and watched. Just as Noah and his sons were finishing the ark, Miriam heard God tell Noah that the rain would start very soon and would not stop for forty days and forty nights. God told them that they would all be safe and dry on the ark.

While Noah and his family were gathering food and water, Miriam and Ezra began to gather the animals. All the animals were very happy to be chosen to be on the ark and were all very kind to each other. From the largest elephant to the tiniest ant, Miriam and Ezra brought animals from every corner of the earth. The animals walked, flew, hopped or slithered their way onto the ark, just as the rain began to fall.

When Miriam and Ezra made sure that Noah and his family, all the food and water and all the pairs of animals were aboard the ark, there was a mighty crash, as God himself closed the ark door, ready for the flood. That was when the rain got very heavy.

Just as God had told Noah, it rained for forty days and forty nights and all of the land disappeared, even the tallest mountains. Every creature, large and small, was warm and dry in the ark. Even when God sent the strong winds to dry up the earth, all of God's creatures were safe aboard the ark.

One day, the ark finally stopped floating and everyone knew that soon, there would be land and that everyone would be able to leave the ark. It was soon after that that Noah called on Miriam again for help. He asked her to fly out and see if it was safe to leave the ark yet. Miriam brought back an olive branch and Noah knew that very soon it would be time to leave the ark.

Sometime later, Noah sent Miriam out again, but this time asked Ezra to go with her and when they did not return, Noah knew that they had found somewhere to land and build a nest. It was time for everyone to leave the ark and find a new home!

The same as the animals came onto the ark, they left, two by two, walking, crawling, flying and slithering. The sun shone down brightly and everyone was happy to see the bright new world that was clean and fresh.

Noah and his family built an altar and as they all knelt down and thanked God for keeping them safe and dry on the ark, Miriam and Ezra flew down to pray with them. They all thanked God for bringing them through the rain to this beautiful new world.

"But when she could no longer hide him, she took an ark of bulrushes for him, daubed it with asphalt and pitch, put the child in it, and laid it in the reeds by the river's bank" EXODUS 2:3

A very long time ago, in fact it was well over 2000 years ago; there lived a curious little Egyptian kitten named Khu.

Khu was a beautiful spotted Egyptian kitten that lived in a palace with the pharaoh's daughter. The name Khu means protected and the princess did her best to keep Khu protected. Unfortunately, Khu liked to sneak out of the palace and scamper through the long grass.

One day, Khu had snuck out of the palace and was prancing through the long grass by the river Nile. The princess was looking for her. Khu didn't care because it was just so nice to be out of the palace in the fresh air.

As Khu got right down by the river Nile, she was discovered by a young girl. The girl stroked Khu's soft, furry back, but she was watching something in the water. Khu then heard a quiet cry, like a baby!

Khu ran off to try to find out where the sound was coming from. That was when the princess discovered Khu. As the princess picked Khu up, the princess also heard the cry of the baby!

The princess ordered one of her servants to walk into the river Nile to find the baby. The baby was tucked in a basket floating on the river. The princess was so excited when her servant brought the basket with the baby back to her! The princess sat down on the edge of the river with the basket. Khu jumped in the basket and curled up next to the baby. The princess was sure that Khu and the baby would be friends forever.

Khu heard the princess ask the servant to find someone to look after the baby until he was old enough to come to the palace. That's when the girl stepped out of the tall grass and told the princess her name was Miriam.

Miriam said she knew someone who would be very happy to look after the baby and return him to the princess at the palace. The princess asked Miriam to get her right away.

While Miriam was gone, Khu heard the princess tell the servants about her father, the pharaoh, who ordered that all baby boys be killed. The princess told them that this baby would be safe and she would not let anything happen to him.

Miriam returned and introduced Jochebed, her mother. Jochebed leaned into the basket and Khu heard her tell the baby she was so happy he was safe! Jochebed said she was so very happy that her son had been found by the daughter of the Pharaoh because he would be well looked after for the rest of his life.

The princess told Jochebed that the baby would be called Moses and that Jochebed was to take the Moses and Khu and look after them both until they could be returned to her to live in the palace.

Jochebed and Miriam returned home carrying Moses and Khu in the basket. What a day it had been! Khu had been able to escape the palace and find a new special friend.

For three years, Jochebed carefully looked after both Moses and Khu. Moses and Khu became great friends and Khu followed Moses wherever he went and slept with him whenever he slept.

It was a very sad day when Jochebed had to take Moses and Khu to the palace. Moses was a beautiful little boy, very strong and wise. Khu was a beautiful cat, with lovely spots and very soft and silky fur. The two were always together.

Jochebed walked very slowly to the palace holding Moses' hand, with Khu following very closely behind. As they walked, Jochebed told Moses the story of the basket in the river Nile and why she had done what she had done. Jochebed said that she knew that it was God himself sent the princess to find Moses.

As Jochebed, Moses and Khu reached the palace; the princess came running out to meet them. She was so excited that Moses was now going to live with her. The princess was also very excited to see Khu again.

The princess thanked Jochebed for bringing Moses to her, and Khu watched as a very sad Jochebed turned to go home, while a very happy princess returned to the palace with Moses followed by Khu. Khu knew that it was a kind and gentle God that would keep them safe.

Khu the protected had now become the protector of Moses!

Didymus the Donkey and Ruth

"So, Naomi returned, and Ruth the Moabitess her daughter-in-law with her, who returned from the country of Moab. Now they came to Bethlehem at the beginning of barley harvest." RUTH 1:22

A very long time ago, in fact it was well over 2000 years ago; there lived a faithful little donkey named Didymus.

Didymus was a small, but strong little brown donkey that belonged to Ruth. Didymus and Ruth were good friends and went almost everywhere together in their little town of Moab.

Didymus liked to go for long walks with Ruth and her husband Mahlon. Sometimes Mahlon's brother Chilion and his wife Orpah would go with them. Didymus liked that they were a very close family, but both Mahlon and Chilion died very young. Didymus found it sad that the father of Mahlon and Chilion had also died very young, leaving their mother Naomi alone.

Although Didymus missed Mahlon and Chilion, he especially enjoyed his time with Ruth and also Orpah and Naomi. One day while Didymus was on a walk with Ruth, Orpah and Naomi, Naomi told them the story of how she came to live in Moab.

Didymus thought it was sad to hear about the great famine in Judah, where the crops could not grow for three years on Naomi's little farm in Bethlehem. Didymus listened as Naomi told Ruth and Orpah that the famine was now over and that she wanted to go home to Bethlehem. Naomi told them that she was not happy living in Moab, where the people prayed to the strange gods of Baal.

Didymus worried that Naomi was too old to take the long walk, so he was very happy when both Ruth and Orpah insisted that they walk with Naomi.

Didymus stood very proudly as Ruth loaded everything they needed to take with them onto his back. Ruth told Didymus that they would be walking for many days before they got to Bethlehem, but Didymus was a strong little donkey.

Didymus was not yet in Bethlehem when Naomi told Ruth and Orpah that she no longer needed them to walk with her. Naomi said she would be fine on her own. Didymus nudged Ruth, who told Naomi that she must stay with her and would pray to the one true God, like Naomi, and not the gods of Baal. Orpah returned to Moab.

When Didymus arrived in Bethlehem with Ruth and Naomi, it was harvest time! Didymus was so happy to hear that it was a tradition for the farmers to leave some fruit on the trees and grain in the fields for the poor to gather. Didymus went with Ruth every day to gather food from the fields.

One day, while Didymus and Ruth were in the field gathering grain, a man came over. Didymus was afraid for Ruth, so he stood between Ruth and the man and watched the man very carefully. His name was Boaz and he owned the farm.

Didymus listened as Ruth told Boaz that she was the daughter-in-law of Naomi and that they had just returned from Moab. Didymus then heard that Boaz was actually a relative of Naomi.

Boaz was even kind enough to give Didymus an apple, so Didymus knew that Boaz was now a friend too. Didymus was even more excited to hear that Boaz would be sure that there would be grain left in the fields to feed not only Ruth and Naomi, but Didymus too!

Almost every day, Boaz would come to chat with Didymus and Ruth in the fields. Didymus could tell that it was really Ruth that Boaz came to see. One day, when Didymus saw Boaz, Didymus could tell that he was especially happy.

Boaz brought Didymus an apple as he often did, but after a quick rub behind his ears, Boaz turned to Ruth. Didymus listened as Boaz told Ruth that he liked her very much and had asked the leaders of Bethlehem if they would give permission for him to marry her and they had agreed! Didymus could tell that Ruth was very excited that Boaz had asked her to marry him.

Didymus watched proudly as Ruth and Boaz were married in the field where they met. Didymus was also very excited when Boaz asked Naomi to come and live with them in his home. Didymus, of course, would now live in the lovely stable with the horses on Boaz's farm. How wonderful for all of them!

Just over a year later, Didymus was so very happy again, when Ruth had a baby boy. Didymus agreed when Naomi said how wonderful it was to have a family and plenty to eat. Didymus knew that it was God who had led them to Bethlehem and to this wonderful new life.

A very long time ago, in fact it was well over 2000 years ago; there lived a very brave little dog named Felix.

Felix was a beautiful little golden dog that took his job as a messenger of God very seriously. The name Felix actually means happy and Felix the dog was very happy. His best friend was Joshua and Joshua was the leader of the Israelites. Felix knew that, because he listened when God spoke.

God spoke to both Felix and Joshua. Felix and Joshua were sent by God, with the other Israelites to live in a land called Canaan.

Just inside Canaan was a big city called Jericho. Jericho was a very strong city with very high walls and very sturdy gates. Joshua needed to take over the city for the Israelites, so Felix stood proudly with Joshua as he spoke to two men, Levi and Gareb.

Joshua needed Levi and Gareb to sneak into the city to see if they could find out how to take it over. Levi and Gareb patted Felix on the head as they left to sneak into Jericho on their mission to discover how to take it over.

Felix and Joshua waited by the warm fire in the Israelites camp a very long time for the men to come back to camp. When Levi and Gareb finally returned, they had a very interesting story to tell. The king of Jericho had heard that the men were sneaking into Jericho and tried to catch them!

Before Levi and Gareb could get caught, Rahab, one of the women of Jericho, hid them in her house. When the king's soldiers came, Rahab told them the men had already left. The soldiers believed her!

Felix nodded while Levi and Gareb told Joshua that Rahab had helped them because God had told her that Joshua and the Israelites were to have the land and take over Jericho. Rahab had asked if the Israelites would please save her and her family when they captured the city of Jericho. Levi and Gareb had told her to leave a red rope in the window, so they would know to protect her house.

Joshua hugged Felix as he told everyone that they would attack Jericho. But first, the Israelites had to cross the great river Jordan. Joshua sent the priests and Felix to the river to start the dangerous journey across. When they got there, the river stopped running! All of the Israelites were able to cross safely and when they got to the other side, the river began to run again.

All of the Israelites cheered! Joshua told them to gather twelve rocks from the river. He told them that each rock would represent one of the twelve tribes of Israel. Felix scampered around everyone as they stacked the rocks up to remind everyone where they had crossed the river.

After the Israelites had gone to sleep for the night, Felix listened as God gave him and Joshua special instructions for the attack on Jericho.

God told them they must march around the walls of Jericho once every day for six days. Seven priests, blowing trumpets would lead them, and everyone but the priests would just march quietly. On the seventh day, they were to march around the city seven times.

Every day for the next six days, Felix marched proudly beside Joshua, with everyone around the great walls of Jericho. The people of Jericho stood on the walls shaking their heads as they watched the Israelites march around the city. On the seventh day, as the Israelites finished their march around the city seven times, the trumpets blew, everyone shouted and Felix barked as loud as he could!

The great walls of Jericho began to crack! Then the earth began to shake! Felix and the Israelites jumped out of the way, just as the great walls of Jericho came crashing down to the ground. Felix, Joshua and all the Israelites ran into the great city of Jericho and captured the whole city!

Levi and Gareb, who had been saved by Rahab, ran through the city to look for the red rope. They took Rahab and her family to the safety of the Israelite camp. Felix knew she was safe because she trusted in God.

Felix and Joshua knew that if you put your trust in God, you would always be safe! It was because they trusted in God that they were able to capture the city of Jericho. Felix scampered around Joshua, knowing that they would all live happily in the Promised Land, if they always believed in God.

Rizpah the Lioness and Daniel

"So the king gave the command, and they brought Daniel and cast him into the den of lions. But the king spoke, saying to Daniel, "Your God, whom you serve continually, He will deliver you."" DANIEL 6:16

A very long time ago, in fact it was well over 2000 years ago; there lived a very kind lioness by the name of Rizpah.

Rizpah lived with a whole pride of lions. In the nice weather, the lions loved to be outside in the bright sunshine, but when it was very sticky and hot or wet and rainy, they went into their den. When they were hungry, they would hunt. The lions would never harm another creature unless they were really hungry.

One day, when it was very hot, they were resting in their den. Rizpah watched as a man was thrown into their den and a big rock was rolled in front of the opening. Thinking that perhaps the man was thrown into their den because he was too hot outside, the other lions settled back down for a nap.

The man seemed very afraid of them, so Rizpah, wandered over to see if she could calm the man down and he told her the most amazing tale.

The man told Rizpah his name was Daniel and he believed in God. Daniel told Rizpah about how kind and wonderful God was and that he prayed to God every day to thank Him for Daniel's many blessings. Daniel also told Rizpah that when he had to, he would also ask for the help of God, and that that was why Daniel had been thrown into the den with the lions.

Rizpah listened as Daniel told her of King Darius. Daniel had been a slave, but because he could interpret dreams, he had become an advisor of the king.

Some of the leaders were very upset about this and didn't want Daniel to advise the king. They knew that Daniel prayed to God to thank him for his blessings, but also to ask for help or guidance. This gave the leaders an idea!

They had told King Darius that anyone who does not go to the king himself for help or guidance should be killed.

Daniel told Rizpah that King Darius thought they must be right and passed a law that anyone asking God instead of the king for anything must be thrown to the lions! Even though Daniel knew about this, he continued to pray to God every day. One day, Daniel prayed to God to help him find a way back to his home land. This was asking God for something rather than asking the king and the leaders heard this and told King Darius.

Daniel told Rizpah that King Darius must now know that the leaders had tricked him into making the law! Rizpah thought the king did not want to harm Daniel because he had become a trusted advisor, but it was the law that Daniel must be thrown to the lions. Daniel told Rizpah that the king had looked very sad as he ordered Daniel to be thrown to the lions.

Rizpah was very surprised and wondered what the king thought the lions were expected to do. Daniel told Rizpah that the king and the leaders believed that lions would eat him!

Rizpah could not believe it! Imagine, lions eating people! Rizpah wanted to make sure that Daniel knew that God's creatures did not harm any other of God's creatures unless they needed food.

To help Daniel understand, she got close to Daniel and nudged his hand. Daniel stroked Rizpah and listened to her purr. Soon Daniel and Rizpah were napping like the other lions. They napped right into the next morning.

Early that morning, like every morning, Daniel said his prayers to God and Rizpah got to listen. As he prayed, he thanked God for keeping him safe with the lions and allowing him to become friends with Rizpah.

Just as Daniel finished his prayers, Rizpah watched as the rock was rolled away from the den and the king himself appeared! The king looked very surprised as the purring lions yawned and stretched next to Daniel. Rizpah listened as Daniel told King Darius that the lions had not hurt him at all. Daniel also told the king that God would not allow any creature to harm another unless they really needed food. King Darius told Daniel that he must find a punishment for the wicked leaders who had tricked him into throwing Daniel into the lion's den.

Rizpah was so happy when King Darius told Daniel that he thought that God was so amazing that he would pass a new law telling his entire kingdom that everyone should pray to Daniel's God, the one true God.

"Now the Lord had prepared a great fish to swallow Jonah. And Jonah was in the belly of the fish three days and three nights" JONAH 1:17

A very long time ago, in fact it was well over 2000 years ago; there lived a huge, great whale named Kish.

Kish liked to wander under the sea and come up to the surface every now and then to see the ships. Sometimes, the sea would be very rough and Kish worried about the ships being tossed to and fro on the top of the sea.

Kish knew that it was dangerous for the ships when the sea was rough. When the sea was especially rough, he made sure he would swim to the surface to see if there was anything he could do to help the ships to be safe.

One day, when the sea was very, very rough, Kish went to the surface just as a man was being thrown overboard! Kish thought this was very strange. The man would not be able to swim in such rough water. Kish had to do something!

As soon as the man landed in the water and began to sink, the seas calmed down and became very flat. Kish dove down and scooped the man up in his huge mouth! He knew he could get him to land, but it would be a long swim because Kish was very far out at sea.

The man's name was Jonah and he believed in God. Kish knew this because as soon as Jonah settled inside his belly, Jonah began to pray. It was through the prayers that Kish could hear the story of how Jonah had been on the ship and why he was thrown into the sea.

Kish listened as Jonah told God that he was sorry that he had been afraid to be a prophet, as God had asked. Jonah had not wanted to go on the long and dangerous journey to Nineveh. He told God that he was also very sorry for getting on the ship that was sailing to Tarshish in Spain, but he had wanted to get as far away from Nineveh as possible and had actually been trying to hide from God.

As one of God's creatures, Kish knew that there was no need to run from God, and you certainly couldn't hide from God. In fact God always knows where you are and He will always be there to help you.

Kish knew Jonah was right when he said to God that he knew when the seas had become very rough, that God was angry because he had tried to run away. Jonah told God that he thought that if the sailors would throw him overboard, he would be able to save the ship and everyone on the ship.

Jonah told God how brave the sailors had been. The sailors had thrown the cargo over first, because Jonah had paid to be on the ship and they didn't think they should throw him overboard even when he asked them too. Jonah asked God to please make sure all the sailors on the ship were safe.

Jonah said to God that he had been afraid for his own life when he was thrown overboard, but he knew it was the only thing he could do. Jonah had been right, the sea had calmed down right away, but now he was in the belly of a whale!

Kish listened as Jonah prayed to God to save him. Jonah promised that if God helped him get back to land, he would do everything God asked him to do. Kish knew that God wanted him to get Jonah to land.

It was very dark and cold and smelly inside the whale Jonah told God, but Jonah knew that since God had kept him safe so far, everything would be okay. He told God that as soon as he was on land again that he would go right to Nineveh and do as God had asked.

Kish carried Jonah for three days and when he finally reached land, he swam up on the beach and spat Jonah out. Jonah thanked Kish for carrying him from the sea to a safe place. But now, Jonah had to help Kish.

Kish was stuck on the beach and Jonah had to help Kish to get back into the sea. Jonah prayed to God for the strength to push Kish back into the sea. Then Jonah pushed and pushed with all his might, and safely got Kish back into the sea. As Kish began to swim away, he sprayed water up through his blow hole and slapped his tail on the water to wish Jonah well.

When Kish turned around to look back at the beach, Jonah waved and smiled his thanks to Kish. Kish was so very happy to help God by getting Jonah safely to land and he knew that as long as Jonah always listened to God and did as he was asked he would always be safe.

CPSIA information can be obtained at www.ICGtesting.com
Printed in the USA
LVOW02s0803030114

367816LV00001B/2/P